Ten Commandments

MARISA BOAN

Copyright 2022 - Ten Commandments by Marisa Boan - Graphics by EduClips
Magic Spells for Teachers LLC - All Rights Reserved

Moses and the Ten Commandments

Moses and the Israelites had been traveling from Egypt through the desert for many months.

When they arrived at Mount Sinai they were tired and hungry.

Moses climbed the mountain to speak to God. He stayed at the top of the mountain for 40 days and 40 nights. God gave Moses the 10 Commandments on stone tablets to share with the people.

The Ten Commandments guide us in making choices that help us to live as God wants us to live.

I am the Lord your God. Thou shall have no other gods before me.

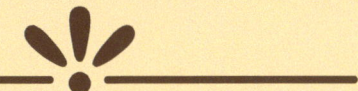

There is only one God.

Love God more than anything else.

Thou shall not take the Lord's name in vain.

Do not swear or misuse the Lord's name, even if you are angry.

Always say God's name with honor and respect.

Remember the Sabbath Day
and keep it holy.

Keep the Sabbath Day holy.

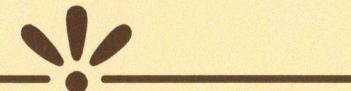

Do not work on the seventh day so that you may worship the Lord on this day.

Honor thy Father and thy Mother.

Love, honor, and respect your parents.

Listen and obey your parents.

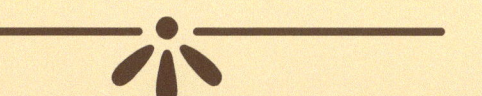

Thou shall not kill.

Respect living things. Do not hurt anyone with actions or words.

Be kind to others at all times. Do not fight or argue with others.

---❋---

Thou shall not commit adultery.

------

Respect your body and others.

Honor the vows you make to each other in front of God.

Thou shall not steal.

Do not take anything that does not belong to you.

Always ask permission before using something that belongs to someone else.

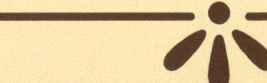

Thou shall not bear false witness against thy neighbor.

Always tell the truth.

Do not tell lies, stories, or gossip about others.

Thou shall not covet thy neighbor's wife.

Do not be jealous or envious of others.

Nothing should come between the love of a husband and wife.

Thou shall not covet thy neighbor's goods.

Do not be jealous or envious of the things that others have.

Do not wish for other people's things. Be happy with the things you have.

Activities for Kids

Cut and Color a Mini Book of the Ten Commandments
Cut out each of the 12 squares and staple them together to form a mini-book. or use them as flashcards.

Matching Commandments
Cut out all of the boxes. Try to match the commandment and the picture.

Commandments Scenarios
Write the name of the Commandment the sentence is referring to.

Moses receives the 10 Commandments

I am the Lord your God. Thou shall have no other gods before me.

Thou shall not take the Lord's name in vain.

Remember the Sabbath Day and to keep it holy.

Honor thy Father and thy Mother.

Thou shall not kill.

Thou shall not commit adultery.

Thou shall not steal.

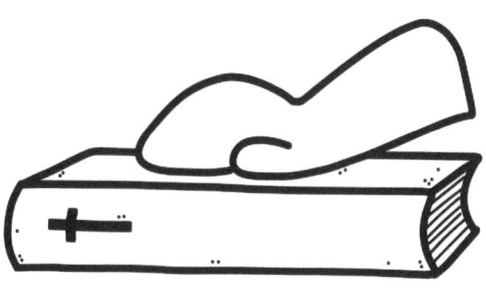

Thou shall not bear false witness against thy neighbor.

Thou shall not covet thy neighbor's wife.

Thou shall not covet thy neighbor's goods.

Matching Commandments

Cut out all of the boxes. Try to match the commandment and the picture.

Thou shall have no other gods before me.	
Thou shall not bear false witness.	
Thou shall not take the Lord's name in vain.	
Thou shall not commit adultery.	
Thou shall not kill.	

Matching Commandments

Cut out all of the boxes. Try to match the commandment and the picture.

Remember the Sabbath Day and keep it holy.	
Thou shall not covet thy neighbor's wife.	
Honor thy Father and thy Mother.	
Thou shall not covet thy neighbor's goods.	
Thou shall not steal.	

Commandment Scenarios

Write the name of the Commandment the sentence is referring to.

I do not have enough money so I want to steal a candy bar.	
I want to say God's name when I am angry with my friend.	
I want to hit my brother for telling on me.	
I want to stay in bed and play video games rather than go to Mass on Sunday morning.	
I did not study and wanted to copy the answers from someone else's test in school.	
I feel jealous that my friend has a new bike and I do not.	

Explore More Books

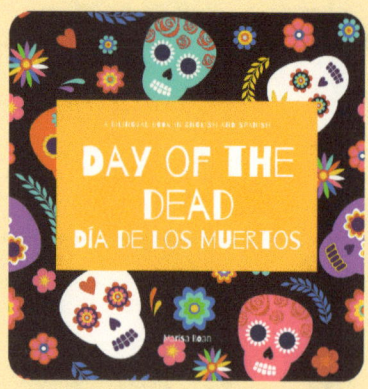  

MAGICSPELLSFORTEACHERS.COM

Available at
amazon

Printed in the USA
CPSIA information can be obtained
at www.ICGtesting.com
LVHW061749031223
765573LV00027B/118